DRUG DANGERS

The Dangers of Methamphetamine

Hal Marcovitz

ReferencePoint Press®

San Diego, CA

ReferencePoint Press®

© 2017 ReferencePoint Press, Inc.
Printed in the United States

For more information, contact:
ReferencePoint Press, Inc.
PO Box 27779
San Diego, CA 92198
www.ReferencePointPress.com

LIBRARY OF CONGRESS CATALOGING-IN-PUBLICATION DATA

Names: Marcovitz, Hal, author.
Title: The dangers of methamphetamine / by Hal Marcovitz.
Description: San Diego, CA : ReferencePoint Press, 2017. | Series: Drug
   dangers | Audience: Grade 9 to 12. | Includes bibliographical references
   and index.
Identifiers: LCCN 2016015863 (print) | LCCN 2016022563 (ebook) | ISBN
   9781682820223 (hardback) | ISBN 9781682820230 (eBook)
Subjects: LCSH: Methamphetamine abuse--Juvenile literature. | Drug
   abuse--Juvenile literature.
Classification: LCC RC568.A45 M37 2017 (print) | LCC RC568.A45 (ebook) | DDC
   362.29/95--dc23
LC record available at https://lccn.loc.gov/2016015863

CONTENTS

CHAPTER 1: How Serious a Problem Is Methamphetamine?

When people visit Indiana, they often find small towns with a quaint midwestern charm, sports fans in love with college basketball, and, each year during Memorial Day weekend, the Indianapolis 500—perhaps the world's most famous auto race. But Indiana also has an unpleasant underbelly: according to law enforcement statistics, it leads the country in illegal methamphetamine labs.

With just 2 percent of the population of the United States, Indiana is home to 15 percent of the country's meth labs—clandestine places where drug dealers cook this dangerous drug. According to the Missouri State Highway Patrol, which compiles national statistics on methamphetamine production, in 2015 police raided nearly thirteen hundred meth labs in Indiana. Undoubtedly, many more continue to operate unknown to law enforcement.

The abundance of meth labs operating in Indiana illustrates that the problem of methamphetamine use is not just limited to the hard city streets in places like New York, Chicago, and Los Angeles. Clearly, methamphetamine is a drug found in small towns and suburban communities too.

A Wide Spectrum of Users

According to the National Institute on Drug Abuse (NIDA), more than 12 million Americans have used methamphetamine at least once in their lifetimes. Moreover, a private drug treatment center, Lighthouse Recovery Institute of Delray Beach, Florida, estimates that some 440,000 Americans are currently addicted to the drug. This is in large part because methamphetamine has emerged as a drug that appeals to people in many age groups as well as wealthy people, poor people, and others who fall in between. As an Illinois judge once observed about the wide cross section of people who have appeared in his courtroom charged with crimes related to methamphetamine use,

It used to be that most of the drug cases were fairly young people. They were people in their teens, twenties, or maybe even some in their thirties. Those were the age groups that were really affected. With methamphetamine we get all ages. We've had people in their sixties. It's quite common to have people in their forties and fifties. It is definitely a drug that cuts across all age groups.[1]

Methamphetamine, also known as crystal meth because of the drug's crystalline appearance, appeals to people of varying ages and incomes.

During the past decade many reports have surfaced about a wide variety of Americans who are methamphetamine users. Certainly, there are many cases that portray the stereotypical drug user: a school dropout, unemployed and living on the streets, surviving on handouts. This person usually resorts to petty crimes to raise the cash he or she needs to buy drugs. The story of a young methamphetamine user named Jasmine is typical. After first trying the drug at the age of thirteen, Jasmine became a regular user. Telling her story on a website maintained by the national drug treatment organization Phoenix House, she says,

> "When I went to court, the judge said, 'I'm locking you up because you look like you're going to die.'"[2]
>
> —Jasmine, a teenage methamphetamine user.

By the time I hit the age of 14, I was heavily into my addiction. I got arrested and went to juvenile hall for assault and battery. When I got out, I was doing drugs while I was on probation. This was the point where I was just doing meth nonstop. I slowed down on drinking and smoking weed just to smoke meth. . . .

By age 16, I was using about $200 worth of meth a day. I was living with a drug dealer, so I didn't have to pay for it. After that, I started going crazy on the people in my life. I threatened my boyfriend that if he didn't give me dope, I was going to do something stupid. Things were really bad, but I kept using. Then, right before I turned 17, I started dealing drugs myself. I got caught with someone on parole in an unregistered car with $90 of dope on me. A couple months after that, I got busted with another parolee for attempt to sell.

When I went to court, the judge said, "I'm locking you up because you look like you're going to die." I had no skin color. I was just skin and bones. That was my rock bottom—pretty much, I was going to die. If I hadn't gotten arrested, I wouldn't be alive right now.[2]

Meth Use Among Young People

Although many people who use methamphetamine begin experimenting with the drug as teenagers, most young people who use illegal drugs do not name meth as their drug of choice. That was the conclusion drawn by the 2014 Monitoring the Future study—the annual University of Michigan assessment of drug use among eighth-, tenth-, and twelfth-grade students.

The Monitoring the Future study found that extremely low numbers of young people admitted to using methamphetamine. The study reported methamphetamine use at 0.6 percent among eighth-grade students, 0.8 percent among tenth-grade students, and 1 percent among twelfth-grade students.

Nevertheless, some young people do use the drug. Young meth addicts say they enjoy the feeling of empowerment—the immense euphoria they experience makes them feel as though they are in charge of their lives. For young people forced to continually follow orders from their parents, teachers, and coaches, methamphetamine often makes them feel as though they are in control. "I just felt invincible," says fifteen-year-old Summers of St. Paul, Minnesota, who first used methamphetamine at the age of thirteen after buying a dose from a friend's drug-dealing brother. "You feel like you're better or stronger than everybody."

Quoted in Martha Irvine, "Teenage Meth Addicts Struggle to Stay Clean," *Los Angeles Times*, April 24, 2005. http://articles.latimes.com.

Users Come from All Walks of Life

But even people who maintain otherwise ordinary lives in comfortable homes can fall victim to methamphetamine use. Elizabeth Fish had carved out a typical middle-class life for herself in Cedar Rapids, Iowa, when she started using methamphetamine. Soon after giving birth to her daughter Cameren, Fish started using meth at the urging of her boyfriend, Derek, and found the drug gave her the energy she needed to keep up with the demands of motherhood:

> A few puffs gave me the energy to clean the apartment, do Cameren's laundry, run some errands, and still be wide awake whenever she cried. I was very careful, though,

never to smoke around Cameren. I'd wait until Derek got home, and the two of us would put our baby down securely in her crib, turn on an air purifier to keep smoke away from her, and go downstairs to light up. I somehow managed to convince myself that by doing it this way, I could take care of my habit—and my baby.[3]

Eventually Fish was arrested for possessing methamphetamine. She was briefly jailed and, faced with the loss of Cameren (and by then a second child), resolved to give up the drug. According to Sheigla Murphy, director of the Center for Substance Abuse Studies at the Institute for Scientific Analysis in San Francisco, Fish's story is typical. "When [mothers] begin to use methamphetamine, they feel more energy, they feel more mastery, they feel like they can get it all done," Murphy says. "They can take care of their kids, they can do their job, sometimes two jobs. They can meet what is for many women today, an almost impossible ideal."[4]

Whether the meth user is more like Jasmine, wandering aimlessly from high to high, or like Fish, using the drug to make raising a family easier, chances are users can be found virtually anywhere in America. One recent study by NIDA attempted to pinpoint the places where meth use is most prevalent, based on the number of seizures of the drug made by police when they arrest dealers or users. The study by NIDA's Community Epidemiology Work Group (CEWP) compared the number of seizures of methamphetamine against the number of seizures of other drugs, such as heroin and cocaine, that occurred in 2013. The study found that the drug is most prevalent in such California cities as San Diego, where 44 percent of drug seizures involved quantities of methamphetamine, as well as San Francisco (39 percent) and Los Angeles (35 percent). Other cities with large percentages of methamphetamine seizures were Minneapolis and St. Paul, Minnesota (33 percent); Phoenix, Arizona (24 percent); Seattle, Washington (24 percent); and Denver, Colorado (22 percent). In contrast, many East Coast cities, among them Boston, New York, Philadelphia, and Baltimore, reported that methamphetamine seizures accounted for less than 1 percent of the illegal drugs seized by police.

Where Are the Meth Labs?

The CEWP study would suggest, then, that methamphetamine use may be most prevalent in the West and Midwest, but other studies have found that methamphetamine use is a problem for most American communities, regardless of geography. The Missouri State Highway Patrol report found meth labs in operation during 2015 in forty-seven of fifty states. And while Indiana led the nation with nearly 1,300 meth labs in 2015, states in the South

Methamphetamine Lab-Related Incidents in the United States, 2014

The US states with the highest number of methamphetamine lab-related incidents in 2014 (the most recent year for which such statistics are available) were Indiana (with 1,471), and Missouri (with 1,034). The numbers reflect incidents involving clandestine meth labs; dumpsites; and related chemical, glassware, and equipment seizures. According to the US Drug Enforcement Administration, the United States as a whole experienced 9,338 such incidents in 2014—down from 12,050 the previous year.

Source: US Drug Enforcement Administration, "Methamphetamine Lab Incidents, 2004–2014." www.dea.gov.

Baseball and Greenies

As methamphetamine emerged as an illegal drug in the 1960s, many people abused amphetamines—the legal form of the drug. Among the abusers were Major League Baseball players. Back in the 1960s and 1970s, long before professional and college sports leagues instituted mandatory drug testing to crack down on steroids and other performance-enhancing drugs, many athletes relied on amphetamines to provide them with extra energy as they competed. In his 1970 best-selling book, *Ball Four*, pitcher Jim Bouton disclosed the widespread use of amphetamines by baseball players, who referred to the drug as "greenies." Bouton wrote,

> Are greenies fabulous? Probably. Some of the guys have to take one just to get their hearts to start beating. I've taken greenies but I think [pitcher] Darrell Brandon is right when he says that the trouble with them is that they make you feel so great that you think you're really smoking the ball even when you're not. They give you a false sense of security. The result is that you . . . throw it down the middle and get clobbered.

> Explaining how players obtained the pills, Bouton wrote, "We get them from players on other teams who have friends who are doctors, or friends who know where to get greenies. One of our lads is going to have a bunch of greenies mailed to him by some of the guys on the Red Sox. And to think you can spend five years in jail for giving your friend a marijuana cigarette."

Jim Bouton, *Ball Four*. New York: Dell, 1970, pp. 146, 159.

and East registered meth lab busts in the hundreds. Among them were South Carolina (586), North Carolina (453), Florida (328), New York (277), and Pennsylvania (247). (The three states that reported no meth lab busts in 2015 were Hawaii, Idaho, and Utah.)

Overall, the Missouri State Highway Patrol reported that the number of meth labs busted by police in 2015 was 7,657. This figure represents a steady decline in meth lab busts since 2010, when 15,337 busts had occurred. However, although the numbers may suggest a 50 percent drop in the number of US meth labs over the course of six years, that statistic does not necessarily mean there is less meth available to American users. For starters, more and more meth is coming over the border from Mexico, meaning homegrown meth labs may be losing business to Mexican drug cartels.

Also, the numbers could suggest that meth lab operators are getting better at concealing their operations, making it harder for police to find them. In fact, officials in Minnesota have reached that conclusion. Police there believe a new trend has started in methamphetamine making: a dealer sets up a lab quickly, makes a batch of the drug, and then moves on to a new location. As Deborah Durkin, a spokesperson for the Minnesota Department of Health, explains, "We don't believe that meth production has decreased, but that meth lab detection is more difficult."[5]

Sergeant Niki Crawford, commander of the Indiana State Police Meth Suppression Section, says the relative ease with which methamphetamine can be made is what sets it apart from other commonly abused drugs such as heroin and cocaine. Indeed, in America virtually anybody can go into the methamphetamine business. According to Crawford, methamphetamine users do not have to rely on their street dealers to supply the drug. If they need meth, she says, they can make it themselves. "Most of our meth cooks are also meth addicts," she says. "This puts meth addicts in a situation where they have total control over their own addiction and the ability to feed their own addiction."[6]

> **"We don't believe that meth production has decreased, but that meth lab detection is more difficult."[5]**
>
> —Deborah Durkin, a spokesperson for the Minnesota Department of Health.

Crystal, Crank, and Ice

Regardless of whether meth is manufactured in a lab in Indiana or in Mexico, on the streets it goes by nearly thirty different names, among them speed, crystal, crank, ice, chalk, and tweak. Moreover, meth can be consumed in a number of ways. Depending on its formulation, methamphetamine can be swallowed in pill form, smoked in a pipe as a powder, snorted up the nose, or injected with a hypodermic needle. Also, powdered quantities of the drug are often wrapped in tiny pieces of toilet paper and then swallowed in a practice known as parachuting. Some users prefer to sprinkle the powdered drug on their fingertips, which they insert into their rectums. According to physicians Malkeet Gupta, Scott Bailey, and Luis M. Lovato in a 2009 report on how users ingest methamphetamine, "The users of this drug are inventive, and almost no method or route of administration goes untested."[7]

In its powdered form, meth is sold in paper packets or plastic bags. It is known as speed or crystal meth when it is swallowed or snorted. Crystal is made in chunks that are clear or yellow, resembling rock candy or rock salt. To snort the drug, the user crushes the crystals into powder. A razor blade is used to create fine lines of the powder, which is then inhaled through a straw or rolled up dollar bill. The drug enters the bloodstream through the vessels in the nostrils.

> "The users of this drug are inventive, and almost no method or route of administration goes untested."[7]
>
> —Physicians Malkeet Gupta, Luis M. Lovato, and Scott Bailey.

When meth is smoked, it is known as ice or glass. The drug is heated in a glass pipe, known in the drug culture as a bong, producing smoke. The smoke is inhaled, entering the bloodstream through the lungs.

Meth is known as crank when it is injected through a hypodermic needle. Users make the drug into a liquid by dissolving the crystals in water. Meth is also made in pill forms. Typically, a pill contains twenty-five or thirty-five milligrams of meth. In recent years drug agents have seized varieties of flavored meth—labs have added vegetable dyes and flavors to the drug in an apparent attempt to lure younger users. One substance is known on the street as strawberry quick because the labs add red dye and strawberry flavoring to the drug. Agents have also seized meth flavored with chocolate and cola.

The Evolution of the Drug

These wide varieties of methamphetamine—crystal, crank, ice, and so on—have their roots in a discovery made in 1887 when Japanese chemist Nagayoshi Nagai extracted a drug known as ephedrine from the ephedra plant. Doctors found ephedrine to be effective in treating asthma, as it helped open constricted bronchial passages. Also in 1887, Romanian chemist Lazar Edeleanu combined ephedrine with other chemicals to synthesize the drug amphetamine. The drug is a stimulant, meaning it can improve mental and physical functions. One early use of amphetamines was to increase blood pressure: patients with irregular heartbeats or weak hearts were prescribed stimulants to improve the heart's ability to beat normally.

Amphetamines work by releasing dopamine, a chemical in the brain known as a neurotransmitter. When released from the brain in large doses, dopamine creates a feeling of euphoria, meaning it makes the person feel good. It also enhances concentration and reduces the need for sleep. During World War I, soldiers were given amphetamines to keep them alert in the trenches. After the war, amphetamines were prescribed for patients with psychiatric disorders. In 1938 the amphetamine Benzedrine went on the market, prescribed by doctors to treat patients suffering from depression. Others who commonly consumed Benzedrine—often known as "bennies"—were long-distance truck drivers, who took the drug to stay awake on the highway, and college students, who stayed awake all night cramming for final examinations. Eventually amphetamines were also used to help people lose weight—a side effect of the drug is appetite suppression.

Amphetamines were widely abused. As a stimulant, amphetamines provide users with enormous reservoirs of pep. The novelist Jack Kerouac wrote *On the Road*, his groundbreaking story of 1950s counterculture, by continually ingesting Benzedrine. Kerouac wrote the novel, which is famous for its stream of consciousness narrative, in just three weeks. "For Kerouac, especially, Benzedrine became an essential component of creativity," says Nicolas Rasmussen, a professor of humanities at the University of New South Wales in Australia. "He wrote on amphetamine to capture raw feelings and experience, the spontaneous 'fresh water' welling up from his unconscious."[8]

Meth and Motorcycle Gangs

Although amphetamines were widely abused, they were legal drugs. During the 1960s amphetamines made the transition to illegal drugs after doctors in San Francisco started to inject heroin addicts with an amphetamine known as Methedrine as a treatment, believing they could be weaned off heroin if they were given amphetamines as a substitute. This therapy had disastrous consequences. Instead, Methedrine provided its own high, and all these doctors succeeded in doing was creating a new population of users who were now addicted to this new drug, which on the street came to be known as methamphetamine.

Illegal dealers found ways to make their own Methedrine in basement labs. In fact, a meth lab could easily be set up for no more than a few hundred dollars in glassware and lab equipment. The drug's main ingredient is pseudoephedrine—a derivative of ephedra found in common over-the-counter cold and allergy medicines, among them Sudafed, Claritin D, and Advil Cold & Sinus.

But pseudoephedrine alone is not sufficient to provide the high sought by drug users. To boost the effects of pseudoephedrine, a meth maker adds a number of toxic chemicals, among them acetone, lye, drain cleaner, ether, battery acid, iodine, paint thin-

Over-the-counter antihistamines like Sudafed contain pseudoephedrine, the main ingredient of methamphetamine.

ner, propane, and ammonia. Most of these ingredients are readily available in grocery stores, drug stores, and hardware stores. They are also highly toxic.

By the late 1960s most methamphetamine sold in America was made and distributed by outlaw motorcycle gangs. Says Richard Valdemar, a former sergeant with the Los Angeles County Sheriff's Department,

> Meth quickly found favor with outlaw motorcycle gangs like the Hells Angels, Banditos, Pagans, and Outlaws. Referred to as "crank" because of the manner in which it was often transported—in Harley-Davidson crankcases—it proved an effective means for ugly bikers to attract young females, who they turned out and used for prostitution, topless dancing, and drug running. Over the years I watched some of these young girls burn out on meth. Within a few years of using the drug they would look like they had aged 20 years, sometimes losing all their teeth and most of their hair.[9]

Government regulators took notice of the widespread abuse of the drug, and in 1970 Congress declared methamphetamine to be an illegal drug. By then, though, the underground meth trade had been established, and the seriousness of America's methamphetamine problem has only grown. In the decades since Congress declared methamphetamine an illegal drug, the substance has become as widely abused as heroin, cocaine, and other substances. Users can be found in big cities, suburban communities, small towns, and rural areas. A drug created to help asthma sufferers breathe normally, soldiers stay awake on the battlefield, and dieters lose weight has evolved into a truly monstrous substance with the ability to completely ruin the lives of its users. "The abuse of methamphetamine—a potent and highly addictive [drug]—remains an extremely serious problem in the United States," says Nora D. Volkow, director of NIDA. "The consequences of methamphetamine abuse are terrible for the individual—psychologically, medically, and socially. . . . Methamphetamine abuse threatens whole communities, causing new waves of crime, unemployment, child neglect or abuse, and other social ills."[10]

CHAPTER 2: What Are the Effects of Methamphetamine Use?

During the 1990s Tom Sizemore forged a Hollywood acting career by playing tough guys in such films as *Saving Private Ryan*, *Natural Born Killers*, and *Pearl Harbor*. He dated beautiful actresses, among them Elizabeth Hurley and Juliette Lewis. He also used heroin and cocaine, but Sizemore was able to kick his addictions and seemed on the verge of major stardom.

In 2001 he started dating a new girlfriend who introduced him to crystal meth. She showed him how to consume the drug by inhaling the powder through a straw. "Ten seconds later, I was flying. . . . I hadn't done coke [cocaine] in years, but this was nothing like coke. It was the most intense thing I'd ever felt," Sizemore recalls. "I was instantly more energetic and euphoric than I'd ever been—it was like hurling forward at the speed of light—and I knew, even though I couldn't admit it at the time, that human beings simply weren't meant to feel *that* good."[11]

Those first few moments of the meth high described by Sizemore are known as the rush—the initial response of overwhelming euphoria the user feels when consuming methamphetamine. During the rush, the user's blood pressure rises and pulse soars. For methamphetamine users, the rush can last as long as thirty minutes.

The high induced by methamphetamine lasts longer than the duration of the rush. In fact, users may find themselves under the influence of the drug for days. But while users may be enjoying their highs, changes are happening that affect their brains and bodies. According to Brett King, a deputy in the Multnomah, Oregon, sheriff's department, "Some people I have in here over a hundred times, and I can look over a 10, 15, 20-year period and see how they've deteriorated, how they've changed. Some were quite attractive when they began to come to jail: young people who were full of health and had everything going for them . . . and now they're a shell of what they once were."[12]

The Shoulder and the Binge

The first phase of the methamphetamine high is followed by what meth users call the shoulder. This period of the high lasts as long as sixteen hours. During the shoulder, the user feels aggressive, smart, and argumentative. Users may speak quickly and finish other people's sentences. There can also be some delusional effects; users have been known to remain focused on insignificant details, sometimes for hours. A meth user may, for example, notice a speck of dirt on a window and spend hours polishing the glass.

That type of activity was typical for Candy Singer, an Oregon lawyer who started using methamphetamine in 2001. Her sister, Thea Singer, describes what Candy was like during the shoulder: "When she was high, which was almost always, she had to be on the computer—diddling with programs to make them run faster, ordering freebies on the Internet. Then computers faded, and she was obsessed with diving into dumpsters—rescuing audio equipment from behind Radio Shack, pens from behind Office Depot."[13]

> "I knew, even though I couldn't admit it at the time, that human beings simply weren't meant to feel *that* good."[11]
>
> —Film actor and former methamphetamine user Tom Sizemore.

Many users continue to ingest methamphetamine while they are still high. This phase is known as the binge, and it can last for days. According to the Los Angeles–based advocacy group Foundation for a Drug-Free World, "During the binge, the abuser becomes hyperactive both mentally and physically. Each time the abuser smokes or injects more of the drug, he experiences another but smaller rush until, finally, there is no rush and no high."[14]

Jack Nagle, a former methamphetamine user from Australia, recalls a binge that lasted nearly two weeks. "I was pale, I was skinny as all hell, I hadn't showered in something like two weeks. I looked like a hobo," he says. During that two-week binge, he

The Damaging Effects of Methamphetamine Use

Meth users experience a variety of damaging health effects. Short-term effects include decreased appetite and increased heart rate and blood pressure. Long-term effects include confusion, paranoia, violent behavior, and ruined teeth. The use of meth during pregnancy endangers not only the woman but also the health of the fetus. And the combination of alcohol and meth can lead to alcohol overdose.

Short-Term	Increased wakefulness and physical activity; decreased appetite; increased breathing, heart rate, blood pressure, temperature; irregular heartbeat.
Long-Term	Anxiety, confusion, insomnia, mood problems, violent behavior, paranoia, hallucinations, delusions, weight loss, severe dental problems ("meth mouth"), intense itching leading to skin sores from scratching.
Other Health-Related Issues	Pregnancy: premature delivery; separation of the placenta from the uterus; low birth weight; lethargy; heart and brain problems. Risk of HIV, hepatitis, and other infectious diseases from shared needles.
In Combination with Alcohol	Masks the depressant effect of alcohol, increasing risk of alcohol overdose; may increase blood pressure and jitters.
Withdrawal Symptoms	Depression, anxiety, tiredness.

Source: National Institute on Drug Abuse, "Commonly Abused Drugs," January 2016. www.drugabuse.gov.

estimates that he used some $5,000 worth of methamphetamine. At the time, he was just twenty years old. He raised the money to feed his binge mostly by stealing. "I started doing things I never thought I would ever do," he says. "Petty crime and things like that. . . . What happens is you lose your grip on reality. Your ability to reason just gets knocked out of the ballpark. . . . Basically you'll do anything to get [meth.]"[15]

During his two-week binge, Nagle says he hallucinated, convinced that he was living his life on a television screen and that everyone was watching him. He also experienced many times during his binge in which he could not remember where he was or what may have happened during those periods. After coming down off his high, his friends told him that he rambled continuously during the binge, often insisting that he was at an airport preparing to board a flight.

The Tweak, the Crash, and the Hangover

Near the end of the binge, the meth user enters a period known as the tweak. At this point, the drug is not providing much of a high and the dopamine stream has virtually stopped flowing. Users find themselves overcome with intense feelings of guilt and loneliness. Sleep is impossible. It is not unusual for users to hallucinate—they see images and hear sounds that are not real. Some users have reported intense itching sensations, as though bugs are crawling over their skin, and they scratch themselves relentlessly. Sarah Cook of Coeur d'Alene, Idaho, whose son is a meth user, says, "He tears his clothes off and ties them around his head. He picks and picks and picks at himself, like there are bugs inside his face. It's Satanic."[16] The Foundation for a Drug-Free World adds that "hallucinations are so vivid that they seem real and, disconnected from reality, [a user] can become hostile and dangerous to himself and others. The potential for self-mutilation is high."[17]

> "He tears his clothes off and ties them around his head. He picks and picks and picks at himself, like there are bugs inside his face. It's Satanic."[16]
>
> —Sarah Cook, a Coeur d'Alene, Idaho, mother describing her son, a methamphetamine user.

After the tweak, the next phase is the crash. As the drug is no longer providing any effect at all, the user's brain and body shut completely down, rendering the user virtually lifeless. During the crash, a user may sleep for as long as three days.

After waking up, the meth user hardly feels rested or invigorated. Rather, the user enters the next phase—the meth hangover. The user is hungry, having not eaten perhaps in days. The body is dehydrated and the user is exhausted, both physically and mentally. During a methamphetamine hangover, many users suffer from severe bouts of depression. A meth hangover can last for as long as two weeks. Yet many meth users do not wait for their hangovers to run their course; instead, they escape the ills of their hangovers by ingesting more meth—and the process begins again.

Meth Mouth and Other Changes

As meth users stay high, or endure life between their highs, changes are occurring in their bodies. The first place where change becomes evident is in the mirror: Meth users often suffer from severe cases of acne because the drug saps moisture from the skin. Moreover, since the drug causes itching, the constant scratching and picking at the scabs by the users damages their skin. Even the youngest meth users tend to form wrinkles common among people decades older. And since they do not sleep or eat regularly, meth users tend to have pale complexions.

"One gentleman I saw said he used it for four months and there was nothing except for root tips left in his mouth."[18]

—Athena Bettger, a Portland, Oregon, dentist who treats inmates at the Multnomah County Prison.

As bad as their skin may look, their mouths look much worse. Meth users often suffer from a condition known as meth mouth: the rotting of teeth and gums. The toxic chemicals used to make meth are known to damage the gums and teeth of users who consume the drug orally, either in pill or powder form. But even meth users who snort the drug or use it via a hypodermic needle are known to suffer from meth mouth. This is because the chemicals used in meth cause a condition known as xerostomia, or dry mouth, which impedes the production of saliva. Xerostomia is regarded as a major cause of tooth decay. Also, the drug tends to lead to a condition known as bruxism, or teeth grinding. Finally, when

Methamphetamine and Pregnancy

If women are pregnant when they use methamphetamine, the health of their unborn babies may be affected. According to NIDA, the babies of mothers who used methamphetamine during their pregnancies are often born premature—meaning their bodies and brains have not had the full opportunity to develop prior to birth. Moreover, babies whose mothers used methamphetamine are often born with lower than normal birth weight. Doctors also have noticed that these babies are lethargic, meaning they do not react normally to sights and sounds. It is also not unusual for babies of meth-using mothers to be born with abnormalities in their hearts and brains.

In 2013 NIDA reported that "a large ongoing NIDA-funded study is examining developmental outcomes in children born to mothers who abused methamphetamine. Thus far, researchers have found neurobehavioral problems such as . . . increased stress and subtle but significant attention impairments in these children."

National Institute on Drug Abuse, "What Are the Risks of Methamphetamine Abuse During Pregnancy?," September 2013. www.drugabuse.gov.

meth users binge, they do not pay much attention to personal hygiene, which means they are not likely to brush their teeth. Athena Bettger, a Portland, Oregon, dentist who treats inmates at the Multnomah County Prison, describes a typical case of meth mouth she encountered: "One gentleman I saw said he used it for four months and there was nothing except for root tips left in his mouth."[18]

Other places where methamphetamine users may suffer ill effects of the drug are in the nose and stomach. As a stimulant, methamphetamine is a vasoconstrictor, meaning it reduces the supply of blood to the place where the drug is administered. Therefore, if a user snorts powdered methamphetamine, the blood vessels in the nose can shrink and become damaged. Tiny sores, known as ulcers, can form inside the nose. Repeated use of the drug can cause the ulcers to bleed. Similarly, taking the drug in pill form can cause stomach ulcers.

Weight Loss and Brain Damage

Meth mouth, acne, scabs, wrinkles, and ulcers can occur within months of a user's introduction to the drug. Other effects occur over the long term, imperiling meth users and, very likely, helping to shorten their lives. Long-term use of the drug can cause atherosclerosis—the development of plaque along the inside of blood vessels. This condition will constrict the blood vessels, which means less blood is flowing to the heart. As such, meth users are at risk for heart attacks.

As a stimulant, methamphetamine is known to suppress appetite. Therefore, when meth users are high, they are not hungry, which means they do not eat regularly. Malnutrition is thus a common malady suffered among users. According to one former methamphetamine user, a nineteen-year-old woman from Kalispell, Montana, "I would stay up for four, five, and six days at a time. I lost 43 pounds in 60 days. I thought I looked beautiful but when I look at pictures from that time, I was hideous."[19]

Meth users may also suffer brain damage that might not become apparent for years. The drug damages brain cells, known as neurons. The neurons do not die; rather, they are pruned back. It means that dopamine and other neurotransmitters do not move freely from neuron to neuron. Since neurotransmitters regulate people's moods and other emotions, the damage to their neurons can have devastating consequences as methamphetamine users age. Users may not be able to think clearly, control their emotions, or even move their limbs. Many methamphetamine users also face memory loss as they grow older.

Steve Wade knows he lost much of his ability to speak, hear, and think clearly because of his heavy meth use. The Spokane, Washington, man had hoped to earn a living as a race car mechanic, but now he spends much of his time in rehabilitation centers, learning how to speak again. Asked what he misses most about his life before he used methamphetamine, Wade stammers, one syllable at a time, "My . . . my brrr-a-i-n. I can't . . . think as clear as I used to."[20] He has difficulty completing sentences and loses his train of thought as he speaks. Moreover, Wade is

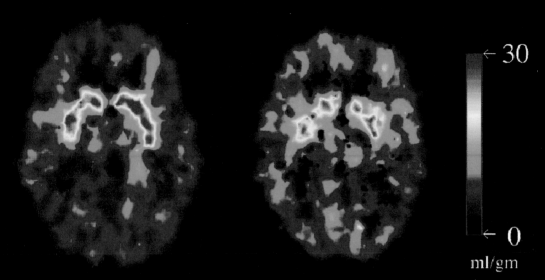

Control Subject   **METH Abuser**

These PET scans, which compare the brain of a meth abuser to that of a control subject, show the damage that results from methamphetamine use. Such brain damage often results in problems with thinking clearly or controlling emotions.

unable to properly care for himself. He cannot shave because his hands shake too much. In addition, he suffers from numerous dizzy spells.

Overdose

Although Wade has lost many of his cognitive functions, he managed to escape his methamphetamine years without suffering the serious consequences of an overdose. A methamphetamine overdose can cause a rapid or irregular heartbeat, skyrocketing blood pressure, and chest pain. Other symptoms are dizziness, nausea, vomiting, diarrhea, and seizures—meaning the user may tremble uncontrollably or find that his or her limbs go rigid. Blood vessels may burst in the body, causing internal bleeding and eventually a stroke—meaning the blood is cut off to parts of the brain, which is a potentially fatal condition. When people survive strokes, they are often disabled for life. Finally, a meth overdose may cause the muscles to go rigid, which can cause a number of organs to shut down, particularly the kidneys. Kidney failure is a potentially life-threatening condition.

James Salant believes he narrowly escaped death after overdosing on methamphetamine, which he had administered through a needle. The dose caused Salant to black out. Sitting on the edge of a bathtub in a friend's house, Salant injected himself, then removed the needle from his arm and placed it on the sink. He felt his head slump. He recalls,

> I lurched forward and didn't fall. My head swung loosely, and drool dropped on the carpet. . . . The difference between life and overdose was not nearly as drastic as I'd assumed. It was like watching a television show attentively and then, while it's still playing, receding into thought. There are lights and noises, and the characters are still talking, but none of it matters. When my head slumped, the world was still there; it just didn't have anything to do with me anymore. . . .
>
> It was only then that I recognized that I wasn't in control. Until then, I had thought that I could come out of it at any time— that I was *choosing* not to wake up and tell everybody that I was okay. But when I tried to tell them that there'd been a ton of speed in the shot I'd taken and that another shot might kill me, I couldn't. It was a struggle to keep my eyes open.[21]

> "Every once in a while somebody had checked my breathing and forced me to open my eyes."[22]
>
> —James Salant, describing his methamphetamine overdose.

Friends discovered Salant slumped over in the bathroom. They threw water into his face and then carried him into the living room. Over the next several hours he wavered in and out of consciousness. "Every once in a while somebody had checked my breathing and forced me to open my eyes,"[22] he says.

Methamphetamine and the Environment

Methamphetamine is made in clandestine labs using a number of toxic ingredients—among them acetone, lye, drain cleaner, ether, battery acid, iodine, paint thinner, propane, and ammonia. Given that there are believed to be more than seventy-six hundred meth labs in operation in the country, a lot of those chemicals are finding their way into the environment. As author David Sheff explains,

> The manufacture of one pound of methamphetamine creates six pounds of corrosive liquids, acid vapors, heavy metals, solvents, and other harmful materials. When these chemicals make contact with the skin or are inhaled, they can cause illness, disfigurement, or death. Lab operators almost always dump the waste. The implications for the Central Valley of California, a source of a large percentage of America's fruits and vegetables—and much of its meth—are significant. In the early 2000s, hospitals in the valley were treating many children, often of undocumented immigrants, for conditions related to the chemical by-products of meth production. As an FBI agent there told me, "Millions of pounds of toxic chemicals are going into the fruit basket of the United States. The chemicals are turning up in alarming levels in ground-water samples."

David Sheff, *Beautiful Boy: A Father's Journey Through His Son's Addiction*. Boston: Mariner, 2008, p. 115.

The Meth Death Toll

Salant's friends were able to revive him, but others who overdose need medical care. According to NIDA, more than 103,000 meth users were treated in hospital emergency rooms in 2011 (the last year for which statistics are available). For thousands of users, medical treatment is not enough—the unfortunate outcome of overdose is death. A 2013 study by the University of Colorado School of Medicine put the number of overdose deaths between 1999 and 2009 at 15,514.

Many local communities compile their own statistics. In 2014, for example, the medical examiner of Pima County in southern

A methamphetamine overdose typically requires emergency medical treatment. In the most recent year for which statistics are available, more than 103,000 meth users were treated in hospital emergency rooms.

Arizona announced that the number of methamphetamine over-dose deaths in the county more than doubled between 2011 and 2013, from thirty-seven to seventy-eight. According to the medical examiner's report, "Methamphetamine was the most commonly abused illicit drug contributing to death in 2013."[23]

Other counties have seen similar spikes in methamphetamine-related deaths. In King County, Washington, the county medical examiner's office reported that seventy people died from meth-amphetamine overdoses in 2014, a 59 percent increase over the prior year, in which forty-four people died. And in San Diego County, California, the US Justice Department reported that the death rate among methamphetamine users nearly doubled between 2009, when 138 people died from overdoses, to 2014, when 262 lost their lives due to methamphetamine overdoses. Dianne Jacob, a San Diego County supervisor, says, "Make no mistake: meth is death, meth breaks lives."[24]

Another way in which methamphetamine can lead to death is through suicide. During the meth hangover, many users suffer periods of devastating depression. People who experience such depression often harbor suicidal thoughts. A 2011 study by Columbia University and the University of British Columbia found that methamphetamine users are 80 percent more likely to take their own lives than users of other drugs, such as heroin and cocaine. One former methamphetamine user who came close to committing suicide was Fred Shafer of Omaha, Nebraska. One morning in 2014, in the throes of a meth hangover, Shafer walked to a bridge over the Missouri River and considered throwing himself into the rushing waters below. "I knew I would die in my addiction," Shafer says. "I would die a junkie. I couldn't go on the way I was."[25] A passerby intervened, and Shafer was eventually able to stay clean.

Shafer and Salant were lucky that their methamphetamine use did not kill them. Wade also made it out of his methamphetamine years with his life, although he will likely never again know the quality of life he enjoyed before he started using meth. The meth rush may provide an enormous sense of euphoria, but those who have tried it often find the ill effects of the substance lasting well after the depression of their meth hangovers goes away.

CHAPTER 3: How Addictive Is Methamphetamine?

Rubetta lives in a small rental house in rural Park Rapids, Minnesota. She is the mother of five children—ranging from two years old to fourteen—but she rarely sees her sons and daughters. Her children live with other family members.

Rubetta cannot care for her children because she is addicted to methamphetamine. A user for twelve years, Rubetta has tried to end her addiction many times but has always failed. She has been arrested numerous times for selling the drug and has been ordered by the courts to undergo treatment for her addiction. She has, admittedly, made little progress:

> When I was . . . coming off a two- or three-day high, and I hadn't gotten any sleep—and I all the sudden got this sense of reality that would kick in and go, "You gotta quit using. OK, I'm gonna." And I was gonna come down, and that would be my last time. And then I'd sleep. And I'd get up and just feel this overwhelming depression—I can't make my breakfast, I can't tie my shoes, I can't take a shower. So all I want to do is hide or sleep. And I was just so depressed coming off that stuff that the only thing that would make me feel better is more.[26]

Among methamphetamine users, Rubetta's story is typical. The drug is regarded as one of the most addictive substances available. "I started using crystal meth when I was a senior in high school," says a young addict who identified herself as Anne Marie. "Before my first semester of college was up, meth became such a big problem that I had to drop out. . . . I spent all my time either doing meth, or trying to get it."[27]

Changes in the Brain

The addictive power of methamphetamine is attributed largely to the chemical makeup of the brain and body. During a meth high, the amount of the pleasure-causing neurotransmitter dopamine is released in a quantity ten times the normal level. The dopamine rush produces an intense feeling of euphoria that users do not want to end—so they use more methamphetamine.

When a person experiments with methamphetamine the first few times, he or she has made a conscious decision to ingest the drug. This decision is made in the part of the brain known as the prefrontal cortex, which regulates voluntary decisions. But meth causes a chemical change in the brain. By the third or fourth use of the drug, the decision to use meth moves into the posterior portion of the brain, a region known as the medulla, which regulates involuntary actions such as breathing. Therefore, the person no longer makes a voluntary decision to use meth—rather, the desire to use meth becomes an involuntary action regulated by the brain. "Meth actually changes your brain," says James Peck, a clinical psychologist at the University of California, Los Angeles. "The brain elevates your need for the drug to the same level as anything else you have to do to survive, like breathing. It starts sending signals saying, 'You have got to get more of that stuff right now.'"[28]

> "I was just so depressed coming off that stuff that the only thing that would make me feel better is more."[26]
>
> —Rubetta, a methamphetamine addict from Park Rapids, Minnesota.

This chemically induced change in the brain happens so quickly that it can turn someone into an addict after just a few uses. "We often see people who've become addicted after one or two uses," says Peck. "It's that powerful." Moreover, Peck says, the meth high is so high, and the low is so low, that the user soon realizes that the only way to escape from the depths of depression common during the meth hangover is to use more meth. "It's like a super-high," Peck says. "And it's like a deep, dark hole of depression when you come down."[29]

Methamphetamine Dependence

Another change in the brain caused by methamphetamine use is that dopamine will not be released into the body without the spark induced by methamphetamine. Before the user started consuming the drug, dopamine could have been released for any number of reasons—for example, after taking a bite of a tasty dessert. Music fans may feel a surge of dopamine when they hear their favorite songs played on the radio. An athlete may experience a dopamine surge after scoring a touchdown or hitting a home run. A student may feel a rush of dopamine after receiving back a test marked with an A. But for the meth user, such feelings are possible *only* under the influence of the drug. In this way, the user becomes dependent on meth.

An addict's dependence on methamphetamine is both physical and psychological. Physical dependence occurs when the user grows accustomed to living constantly under the influence of methamphetamine. When the addict stops using the drug, he or she experiences withdrawal symptoms, including fatigue, depression, and irritability. Users also become disoriented. Moreover, they develop a physical craving for the drug—only by using the drug again can the user feel better.

Addicts also develop a psychological dependence on meth. This occurs because the desire to use the drug becomes more important to them than anything else in their lives—even eating and sleeping. Indeed, methamphetamine addicts become apathetic: they stop caring about their responsibilities and relationships. They simply put obtaining and using the drug above all other activities in life. "Even though [methamphetamine] causes problems in a person's health, daily function, or other important aspects of life, the addict is unable to stop using it," explains Steven J. Lee, a New York City psychiatrist who specializes in addiction treatment. "The fundamental concept of substance dependence is that a person no longer has control of the drug or the use of it—rather, the drug is controlling the person, whether by psychological or physiological means. Despite the growing problems the drug creates, the addict continues to use or increase the amount and frequency of use."[30]

> "We often see people who've become addicted after one or two uses. It's that powerful."[29]
>
> —James Peck, a clinical psychologist at the University of California, Los Angeles.

As the addict develops physical and psychological dependencies on the drug, over time the brain also builds up a tolerance for it. In other words, as the addict continues to use the drug, it takes more and more of it to provide the same high. This occurs because meth causes a change in the user's brain cells, making it harder for the neurons to recharge their supplies of dopamine. It means that as addicts use more and more methamphetamine, it becomes more difficult for their brains to manufacture dopamine. Therefore, meth addicts must take larger and larger doses of the drug to achieve the same effect. "The process is known as tolerance, and with methamphetamine tolerance develops very quickly,"[31] says Ralph A. Weisheit, a professor of criminal justice at Illinois State University.

Walking Away from Their Lives

As they grow dependent on methamphetamine, addicts are known to give up everything to pursue their addiction. Tom Sizemore, the actor, all but gave up a promising film career in search of his next high. In 2003 Sizemore's girlfriend, the one who had introduced him to meth, alleged that he physically assaulted her—a charge he denied. Nevertheless, he was convicted and sent to jail. "I had a

Methamphetamine and Crime

In Ceres, California, police have noticed the regular occurrence of a most unusual crime: the theft of manhole covers. "We lose five to ten manhole covers a week," says Ceres police chief Art de Werk, who believes the thefts are largely committed by methamphetamine users who sell the manhole covers as scrap metal, then use their profits to buy drugs. De Werk's belief is shared by many other law enforcement officials, who suggest that many property crimes, such as thefts and burglaries, are committed by meth users who have turned to crime to raise money to feed their addiction. "It drives more crime than other drugs do," says Margaret Mims, sheriff of Fresno County, California. "Meth is in its own category, because it's so much more addictive than other drugs."

Police departments generally do not keep statistics on which crimes are related specifically to which drugs, but many law enforcement officials do point to meth as a direct cause of many crimes. A 2012 study by the Oregon High Intensity Drug Trafficking Program found that 78 percent of Oregon police officers believe methamphetamine addicts commit most property crimes, such as burglaries and thefts, to raise money for their drug habits.

Quoted in Gosia Wozniacka and Tracie Cone, "Horrific Murder No Surprise in US Meth Hub," NBC News, January 21, 2012. www.nbcnews.com.

home, cars—all this stuff that it had taken a long time to accumulate. I thought, 'There's no way I could lose it all.' But within three years, it was gone."[32] And even after his release from jail, Sizemore still used methamphetamine.

Sizemore was a celebrity and had a lot to lose—his movie career, a sizable bank account, and the lifestyle of the rich and famous. However, others of more modest means are just as willing to walk away from their lives, giving up school, jobs, and relationships all in pursuit of the next rush. Moreover, they put family members through intense grief as they turn away from loved ones. When they burn through their savings, they often turn to panhandling or crime to finance their addictions.

> "All my dreams, my hopes, ambitions, relationships—they all fell away as I took more and more crystal up my nose."[33]
>
> —Former methamphetamine addict Nic Sheff.

Growing up in San Francisco, Nic Sheff started using the drug when he was eighteen years old. An athlete and honor student in high school, all his achievements meant little to him as he relentlessly pursued meth. Describing what life was like as he became addicted to the drug, Sheff says,

> All my dreams, my hopes, ambitions, relationships—they all fell away as I took more and more crystal up my nose. I dropped out of college twice, my parents kicked me out, and, basically, my life unraveled. I broke into their house—I would steal checks from my father and write them out to myself to pay for my habit. When I had a job at a coffee shop, I stole hundreds of dollars from the register. Eventually I got arrested for a possession charge. My little brother and sister watched me get carted away in handcuffs. When my then seven-year-old brother tried to protect me, running to grab me from the armed policemen, they screamed for him to "get back." His small body crumpled on the asphalt and he burst into body-shaking tears, gasping for breath.[33]

An Expensive Habit

Like Sheff, many users steal money to feed their habit because a methamphetamine addiction is a very expensive habit to maintain. Users typically start out with a dose of fifteen milligrams. According to the US Justice Department, one gram of powdered meth can cost between $20 and $150—depending, of course, on its potency. Thus, for as little as $20, a meth addict can obtain enough powder to provide six or seven hits.

Twenty dollars may not sound like much money, but meth addicts burn through money quickly in their quest to remain high. Sheff recalls that during his years of addiction, he committed petty crimes, borrowed money from others, begged on the streets, and sold his possessions—all to raise money to sustain his habit. Living with his girlfriend, Zelda, in a Los Angeles apartment, Sheff says the couple sold their furniture, albums, and even Zelda's diamond wedding ring from her former marriage, all to raise money for drugs. "We're basically out of money," Sheff said at the low point of his addiction. "I'm not sure how we're going to pay the rent, or eat, or anything. I have this hope that maybe I can get a job, somehow, but that is fleeting."[34]

Of course, fifteen milligrams is usually a beginner's dose. As their tolerance grows, addicts find they need larger and larger doses to achieve the highs they desire. That means they are constantly in need of money to buy the amount of drug they need to satisfy their dependency. James Salant is another meth addict who found himself constantly in need of money to feed his growing habit. Salant grew up in a prosperous home—his father is a physician. But Salant turned to drug dealing, selling methamphetamine to his friends, and even resorted to picking through people's trash, looking for items he could resell so he could buy methamphetamine.

Salant says he often accompanied a friend named Patti on such scavenging missions. On one occasion, he says, the two drove through a prosperous neighborhood in Patti's pickup truck as she collected what he thought were trash bags from the curbs by people's driveways. Looking through the bags while Patti tossed them into the back of her truck, Salant noticed the clothes and shoes inside were in fairly good condition. He quickly real-

Even though dealers may charge only a few dollars for a dose of meth, addicts quickly find themselves spending almost all their money in order to satisfy their need for the drug.

ized that Patti was stealing donations that neighbors had placed at the curbside for collection by a charity. "Patti, I think those are donations," Salant says he told his friend. "I think so, too,"[35] she replied. It was clear, Salant said, that Patti had no intention of turning the bags over to a charity. She intended to sell them and use the money to buy methamphetamine.

Cockroaches and Chemicals

Patti's home was always full of the trash she collected as she scrounged for items worth selling. In fact, places where methamphetamine users live are often poorly kept. Meth addicts seldom bother with housecleaning, personal hygiene, or keeping fresh food in the refrigerator—all those responsibilities are forgotten as they search for their next dose of meth.

The overwhelming urge to satisfy their need for meth leads addicts to neglect even basic housekeeping chores.

Indeed, all their responsibilities are forgotten as they seek to remain high. If they have jobs, they do not go to work. If they have classes, they stay home. The only reason most addicts find to leave home is if they run out of meth and need to find the drug elsewhere. Truck driver David Parnell and his wife, Amy, residents of the small town of Dresden, Tennessee, were both methamphetamine addicts. During the years they used, Parnell says they neglected their children and their home. He describes what life was like when the couple binged on methamphetamine:

The laundry didn't get done, the house was filthy, and the kids didn't get bathed. . . . In homes where meth is manufactured, there usually aren't cockroaches. It's not because they can't handle the chemicals in the air—a roach can live through a nuclear bomb—it's because there's no food to eat in the house. On the other side, I've been in houses where I'd hear a thump and see roaches literally falling off the ceiling onto the kitchen counter. We didn't care, though, we were all busy smoking crank. It's disturbing to think that innocent children live in those houses.

Our kids missed a lot of school, but Amy managed to get them on the school bus most of the time. She wanted them out of the house so she could do her drugs in peace. Amy became a shut-in; she never left the house, not even for school functions. As a trucker I was gone for days at a time, and when I wasn't working, I'd be out looking for dope. Amy didn't have any friends or look forward to anything except getting high.[36]

Living in Squalor

Most methamphetamine addicts do not wash dishes. They do not do laundry, change their babies' diapers, or make sure fresh food is in the refrigerator. One such home was discovered in Palisades, Iowa, when police raided an apartment occupied by Nathan Saffer, age twenty-nine; Kerry Hawkins, age twenty-four; and their two young daughters, ages two years and three months. During the raid on the apartment, police found loaded syringes on countertops. "This apartment was not fit for humans to reside in," one officer wrote in his report. "I observed the odor inside the apartment to be overwhelming and unbearable." The officer added that he found the baby's fecal matter on a bedroom floor.

His report continued: "I observed food on the floor everywhere. I observed old food in the kitchen which had been there so long it began to pile up under the cabinets. . . . I did not observe any clean clothing in the apartment for the children." Saffer and Hawkins were arrested and charged with the possession and sale of methamphetamine as well as conspiracy and child abuse.

Quoted in Paul Shockley, "Drug Cops: Children Found in Squalid Meth Apartment," *Grand Junction (CO) Daily Sentinel*, October 22, 2011. www.gjsentinel.com.

An Overwhelming Grip on Their Lives

The Parnells admitted to paying scant attention to their children. However, Sara Kiser and Douglas Bokker were even less focused on the welfare of their child. Both methamphetamine users, this couple from Forrest City, Arkansas, was arrested in 2015 and charged with the murder of their eleven-month-old daughter, Luceilla Bokker. An autopsy revealed that the baby had ingested methamphetamine before she died. Police surmised the child had found the drug while crawling around the house and consumed it. "We do know . . . that both parents use meth," said Bobby May, sheriff of St. Francis County, Arkansas. "We just don't know how the baby got meth into its system."[37]

> "While we were on a binge, the laundry didn't get done, the house was filthy, and the kids didn't get bathed."[36]
>
> —Former methamphetamine addict David Parnell.

Luceilla's death illustrates the depths to which methamphetamine users fall as they feed their addiction. Kiser and Bokker are suspected of leaving methamphetamine in a place, possibly the floor, where their daughter could have placed the powder in her mouth. Sadly, Bokker and Kiser may be typical meth addicts. All other matters in life—their responsibilities and relationships, even the welfare of their children—mean little to them as they constantly search for their next high. Because methamphetamine changes their brains and causes physical and psychological dependencies, few meth addicts have the ability to withstand the overwhelming grip the drug has over their lives.

CHAPTER 4: What Are the Challenges of Treating Methamphetamine Addiction?

Tom Sizemore was sentenced to six months in prison after he was convicted of assaulting his girlfriend, but the judge promised to reduce his sentence by half if he entered a drug rehabilitation center. Sizemore consented and checked himself into Rancho L'Abri, a residential drug treatment center near San Diego. The first night he was at Rancho L'Abri, he swallowed some methamphetamine he had smuggled into his room.

Security was tight at Rancho L'Abri, but Sizemore was able to slip drugs past the guards by hiding them in some loose pieces of paper he had stuffed into his suitcase. After swallowing a dose in his room, Sizemore wandered outside. He saw guards on patrol but slipped by them, then climbed over the fence. He walked 9 miles (14 km) to a highway and then called a limousine service to pick him up. As he was driven to his home in the upscale Benedict Canyon neighborhood of Los Angeles, Sizemore took more meth. He recalls,

> When I woke up the next morning and remembered what I'd done, I almost had a heart attack. I thought I was going to prison. I called Rose, the administrator at Rancho L'Abri, and she said, "Get back here right away." So I went back. And then, three days later, I did the same thing: climbed the fence, called the driver, walked the nine miles, and went all the way home to Benedict Canyon. But this time when I called, Rose said, "If you leave again, you can't come back and you're going to go to prison."[38]

This time, Sizemore behaved himself. He remained at Rancho L'Abri for fifty-seven days—but it still was not enough. "After I was released, I got high yet again," he says. "I'd learned nothing. I still had money and I was an arrogant fool. And I didn't realize how altered my reasoning had become."[39]

"A Pretty Horrible State"

Sizemore's story illustrates the enormous challenges methamphetamine users face when they try to kick their addiction. Meth addicts like Sizemore learn very early in their rehabilitation that the drug has a very strong grip on their life and that relapses are common. "I've seen meth addicts who've been clean ten years get

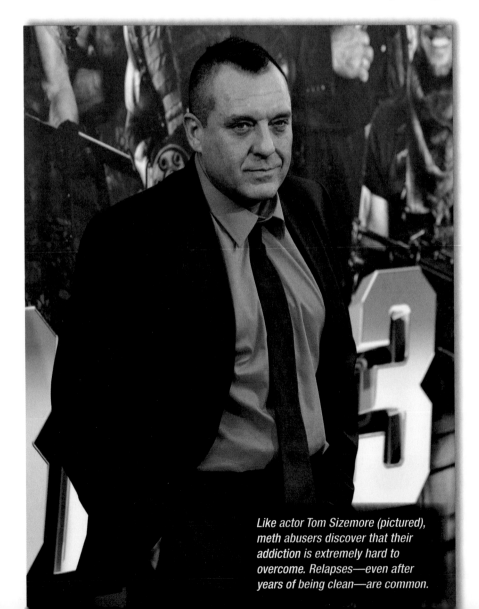

Like actor Tom Sizemore (pictured), meth abusers discover that their addiction is extremely hard to overcome. Relapses—even after years of being clean—are common.

pulled back in," says Ray Framstad, a drug enforcement agent in Merced, California. "The smallest thing can trigger it and take you right back. It's just that powerful."[40]

The first part of overcoming a meth addiction is to persevere through the withdrawal phase. Typically lasting from thirty to ninety days, withdrawal is the period in which the user comes to terms with the hard road ahead. The craving for the drug is intense, and feelings of depression persist. Many meth users have suicidal thoughts during withdrawal. For many others, their solution is to return to using the drug. According to the Foundation for a Drug-Free World, 93 percent of methamphetamine addicts use the drug again during the withdrawal phase.

> "The smallest thing can trigger it and take you right back. It's just that powerful."[40]
>
> —Ray Framstad, a drug enforcement agent in Merced, California.

Among addicts, these feelings can be attributed to the changes that have occurred in their bodies during the months or years of drug abuse. During their addiction, meth has altered their brain chemistry—the pleasure-causing neurotransmitter dopamine is released only through use of the drug. Once the drug is cut off, so is the dopamine, meaning nothing in life is likely to provide pleasure to the recovering addict. This condition is known as anhedonia—the inability to experience enjoyment.

Adi Jaffe reports that anhedonia can be a fairly long-lasting condition that many users find extremely difficult to experience. A former meth addict who kicked his habit and then went on to earn a doctorate degree in psychology, Jaffe now counsels users and helps them kick their own addictions. "Anhedonia doesn't make you throw up and sweat, but it's a pretty horrible state to be in," he explains. "Things that bring a smile to a normal person's face just don't work on most crystal meth addicts who are new to recovery. As if that wasn't bad enough, it can take as long as two years of staying clean for the dopamine function of an ex meth-addict to look anything like a normal person's."[41]

Moreover, many researchers believe that former users will never be able to fully experience normal feelings of pleasure because the drug destroys the dopamine receptors in the brain's neurons.

The portions of the brain cells that help pass the neurotransmitter from cell to cell become permanently damaged; as such, the brain is physically incapable of delivering a normal amount of dopamine to the body through natural means. "It's not just that you lose brain cells and you keep living happily ever after; it translates into a disruption in your performance,"[42] says Nora D. Volkow of NIDA.

Constant Supervision

Since methamphetamine addiction is so gripping, and since recovery from the drug can be so arduous and depressing, experts agree that recovering addicts need to be treated in residential facilities where they can be constantly supervised. Typically, a residential treatment center is as Sizemore described—a high-security facility designed to keep the patients inside. Residents receive around-the-clock attention by staff members. In contrast, recovering addicts who are treated in outpatient facilities are free to return home at the end of the day. Typically, meth addicts who are nearing the end of their treatment transition to outpatient facilities—by then they have gained more control over their addiction and can be trusted to remain off the drug without being constantly monitored.

> "Things that bring a smile to a normal person's face just don't work on most crystal meth addicts who are new to recovery."[41]
>
> —Psychologist and former methamphetamine addict Adi Jaffe.

For the newly recovering addict, however, constant supervision is regarded as a necessity because it is within the first few days or weeks of treatment that many addicts are most likely to lapse back into meth use. "That's when they are at their worst," says Michael Liepman, a psychiatrist and medical director of the Jim Gilmore Jr. Treatment Center in Kalamazoo, Michigan. "They can be irritable, agitated, anxious, confused, angry and paranoid and show impaired judgment."[43] Indeed, as they endure little but sorrow in their lives, they may find themselves drawn back to methamphetamine as a release from the throes of constant depression.

Cognitive Behavioral Therapy

Users of heroin experience similar states of bleakness and depression when they enter rehabilitation. In their cases, however, they can be prescribed legal drugs that help wean them off heroin. For example, the drug methadone has been prescribed to recovering heroin addicts for decades—it reduces the user's craving to get high. Also, if an addict lapses back to heroin during rehabilitation, the methadone blocks some degree of the narcotic effect of the drug, meaning the heroin user feels less of a high. Over time,

Drugs for Methamphetamine Recovery

Although there are no drugs that can currently be used to help wean addicts off of methamphetamine, by 2016 a number of drugs were undergoing clinical trials, meaning they were being administered to a handful of addicts on a test basis. If the trials prove successful, it is possible that the US Food and Drug Administration, which oversees prescription drug development, could approve them for widespread use. "In our pipeline right now, we have about 10 compounds in various stages of clinical trials, most of them very early on, for methamphetamine addiction," says Timothy Condon, the associate director for science policy at NIDA. "They're all classic medications used in other areas of medicine that we're testing as anti-methamphetamine agents."

One medication under study is tyrosine, an amino acid that helps the brain manufacture dopamine, the pleasure-causing chemical that all but disappears when an addict stops using methamphetamine. Another medication undergoing clinical trial is bupropion, which helps smokers kick their nicotine habits. The drug is a mild antidepressant, meaning it helps smokers feel better and, therefore, less likely to use tobacco. Doctors hope it could have a similar effect on methamphetamine users. Also, some researchers are prescribing large doses of vitamin E to former methamphetamine addicts in clinical trials; vitamin E is believed to be helpful in restoring brain cells, which can be damaged through methamphetamine use.

Quoted in Julia Sommerfeld, "Beating an Addiction to Meth," NBC News, 2013. www.nbcnews.com.

doses of methadone administered to the heroin user are reduced until, ideally, the user has overcome his or her addiction.

No such substitute drugs are available for methamphetamine addicts, however. No drug has yet been created that replaces methamphetamine, safely enhancing the release of dopamine. So, to kick their habit, users may undergo a treatment known as cognitive behavioral therapy. This involves retraining the brain to function without needing a meth-induced dopamine rush.

Cognitive behavioral therapy has been used for many years to treat people with certain mental illnesses—particularly phobias. For example, a person who suffers from acrophobia—a fear of heights—may be afraid to take an elevator to the upper floors of a skyscraper. Cognitive behavioral therapy encourages the patient to take small steps toward conquering that fear: For the first few days, the patient is encouraged by a therapist to ride the elevator to the second floor. The next step is to ride the elevator to the third floor and so on until the patient has the confidence to ride the elevator all the way to the top. Along the way, the patient overcomes his or her fear of heights.

Addicts find that a therapist can help them identify and avoid the triggers that cause a renewed craving for methamphetamine.

Using similar techniques, cognitive behavioral therapy can help meth addicts find ways to resist the drug by teaching them to recognize what triggers their desire to get high and then find ways to avoid the triggers. "One of the most important goals of treatment is helping patients identify and avoid triggers, the people, places, things, and situations that can ignite a sudden craving for meth," says Chris Woolston, a biologist and science writer. In many cases the triggers are very evident, such as situations that cause the user stress or former friends of the addict who continue to use the drug. Often the recovering addict knows that when he or she spends time with friends, they invariably use drugs. Therefore, when methamphetamine addicts resolve to give up the drug, they often have to give up their friends as well. "Recovering addicts have found that going to places where they used to get high or hanging out with friends who still use meth are often surefire recipes for relapse,"[44] explains Woolston.

> "Recovering addicts have found that going to places where they used to get high or hanging out with friends who still use meth are often surefire recipes for relapse."[44]
>
> —Chris Woolston, a biologist and science writer.

Subtle Triggers

In other cases the triggers may be more subtle. Certain odors, for example, may remind recovering meth addicts of places where they took drugs, such as the homes of friends who cooked meth in their basements. Since methamphetamine contains many ingredients found in grocery stores or hardware stores—such as drain cleaner, paint thinner, propane, and ammonia—these odors could similarly trigger a craving for the drug. Drug counselors work with recovering addicts to help them recognize those odors and other triggering stimuli and devise ways to avoid them.

Woolston says one common trigger for many meth addicts in recovery is the sight of cash. This is because at the height of their addiction, they tended to be in constant need of cash to buy drugs, and when they did get their hands on some, they invariably spent it on meth. Therefore, a drug counselor must—at least in the early stages of recovery—find ways to keep former users from handling cash.

Sounds—particularly music—can also be a trigger. As he went through cognitive behavioral therapy, Nic Sheff recalled that some of his friends enjoyed listening to the San Francisco–based ensemble Kronos Quartet while using meth. When Sheff entered rehabilitation he disclosed this fact to his counselor, who urged him to avoid the quartet's music. "[The music] made him want to get high,"[45] says Sheff's father, David.

The process of recognizing triggers and finding ways to avoid them can take many months as counselors slowly learn about the individual and what causes him or her to want to use methamphetamine. If the rehabilitation is successful, the triggers are gradually recognized and the recovering user finds ways to avoid them. "The idea is that any behavior, including behavior that seems automatic or compulsive, can become conscious and can then be interpreted," says David Sheff. "Time in treatment—time measured in many months if not years—is usually required for dramatic change. In the process, the user's brain is probably regenerating, and dopamine levels may be normalizing. A cycle of abstinence replaces a cycle of addiction."[46]

Movie Tickets and Meals Out

As the counselor works with the recovering addict to recognize and avoid the triggers that prompt drug use, additional methods and therapies are applied. For example, the counselor looks for ways to improve the addict's motivation for recovery. This is an important step in addiction treatment—and particularly with treatment for meth addiction—because the user is typically depressed and therefore lacking motivation. Many counselors attempt to motivate recovering users by showing them how the drug is destroying their lives—how it has affected relationships with family members and how it has taken a physical toll on them.

Drug counselors also provide incentives—rewards for not using drugs. During recovery, the drug counselor may reward recovering addicts for a drug-free month by giving them movie tickets

Recovering from Methamphetamine Addiction

Heather Porter, a sixteen-year-old former methamphetamine user from Easley, South Carolina, says a drug rehabilitation program helped her learn to resist the temptation to use the drug. According to Porter, she started using the drug while attending high school. "Soon I was snorting dope every day," she says. "My grades dropped from B's and C's to F's, then I stopped going to school altogether. I eventually got kicked out, but I didn't care. My parents, however, were really upset. My dad and I never used to fight. Now all we did was scream at each other."

Porter was arrested for shoplifting in December 2004. The judge sent her to a drug treatment facility for fifty days. "In rehab, I learned how to deal with my problems," she says.

> I was really angry before I started using, and meth only made it worse. But I discovered I have a lot of potential, and I don't need meth anymore. My parents and counselor told me that they had faith in me to be strong. Four days after returning home, I ran into some friends who asked if I wanted to get high. I was proud of myself for saying no. I get tempted, but now I say, "It's not for me."

Quoted in Stephanie Booth et al. "The Faces of Meth," *Teen People*, March 2006, p. 114.

or restaurant coupons. A night out at the movies or at a restaurant may seem like small rewards for the hard work that goes into staying off a highly addictive drug like meth, but for somebody cooped up in a drug treatment facility for what seems like an endless amount of time, an evening away can truly be a rewarding experience.

Family members are encouraged to visit the recovering addict in rehabilitation and provide support. Many times, the family members will be invited to participate in the therapy sessions so they can gain better insight into why their loved ones turned to drugs. Family members can also learn to recognize an addict's triggers. This type of knowledge can be valuable when the recovering addict returns home.

Halfway Houses

After what could be several months in a residential treatment center, some recovering addicts return home while others go to what are known as halfway houses, also called clean-and-sober housing. These are also residential facilities, but recovering addicts are not under twenty-four-hour supervision. Instead, many of them leave during the day to go to work or attend high school or college classes. Back in the center, they undergo counseling and are subjected to constant drug testing, which is conducted through urine samples.

After his release from residential treatment, Nic Sheff lived for several months in Herbert House, a halfway house—actually, a group of bungalows—in Culver City, California. The small houses surround a central courtyard featuring palm trees, picnic tables, and garden furniture. While staying at Herbert House, Sheff found a job working as an aide for a residential drug treatment center in Los Angeles. His job required him to drive patients to meetings with doctors and counselors, help dispense medication, and generally act as a role model, telling other patients his story so they could learn from his experience. David Sheff recalls picking up Nic at Herbert House to help him celebrate his twenty-first birthday: "It is a warm summer afternoon when I picked him up in front of Herbert House. Nic leaps into the car. We hug. He appears whole again. Twenty-one is a milestone in everybody's life, and it is a milestone for parents when their children turn twenty-one. For me, it feels like another miracle."[47]

> "It is a warm summer afternoon when I picked him up in front of Herbert House. Nic leaps into the car. We hug. He appears whole again."[47]
>
> —David Sheff, father of former addict Nic Sheff.

When recovering methamphetamine addicts finally leave residential treatment or halfway houses and move back in with family members or re-establish their own homes, they may still need a degree of rehabilitative therapy. This is provided through outpatient facilities. Typically, the recovering addict may be asked to attend therapy sessions at the outpatient center two or three days a week over a period of three months to as long as a year. In outpatient treatment, the recovering addict continues to engage in cognitive behavioral therapy, learning about his or her personal meth triggers and how to avoid them. "By analyzing their triggers, deciding on recovery-oriented responses and strategies, and role playing high-risk situations and responses, clients gain confidence that they can resist triggered urges to use substances,"[48] reported a 2006 study on outpatient drug therapy by the US Substance Abuse and Mental Health Services Administration.

Moreover, after leaving residential facilities, recovering addicts are encouraged to continue their treatments by joining Narcotics Anonymous and similar support programs. These groups meet regularly— weekly or more often—and provide a place where members can discuss the challenges involved in staying off drugs. They share stories and victories and give each other encouragement and support. They are also paired with mentors, also known as sponsors, who are themselves recovering addicts who have been drug-free for years. The mentors develop one-on-one relationships with their charges, helping them through the rough patches of recovery.

Recovering meth addicts often find that group counseling offered by support programs like Narcotics Anonymous helps them stay clean.

Relapses Are Common

Despite the attention that recovering addicts receive during rehabilitation, the unfortunate truth is that methamphetamine recovery programs have high failure rates. In 2013 the Matrix Institute, a nonprofit addiction research organization in Los Angeles, reported the results of a study that found that 40 to 50 percent of methamphetamine addicts treated with cognitive behavioral therapy return to using the drug after a year. (The Matrix Institute noted, however, that the failure rate for methamphetamine users is similar to the failure rate for cocaine addicts as well as heroin addicts who are not administered methadone.)

This high failure rate illustrates the fact that kicking a methamphetamine habit is a grave challenge, and one the recovering user must spend a lifetime meeting. Tom Sizemore is a perfect example of this. As he fell deeper into methamphetamine addiction, Sizemore continued to win acting roles, but his career began to suffer as film producers found him unreliable. After serving the brief prison term in 2004 for assaulting his girlfriend, Sizemore was arrested again in 2007 for possession of methamphetamine. He was forced to serve another prison term. Even after his release from his second jail sentence, Sizemore lapsed back into meth use and continued taking the drug for another year. He re-entered drug rehabilitation in 2008 and, since then, has managed to remain clean.

Now in his fifties, Sizemore plays mostly supporting roles; he lost the opportunity to move up to leading roles because he spent his prime years as an actor feeding his meth addiction. "The work is coming and it's coming fast—just like it did in the beginning of my career," he says. "They may not all be my dream movies but I get that I'm rebuilding what I lost and that it doesn't all materialize in an instant. That's probably for the best. A slow build means that if I do eventually get everything back, I'll be able to understand and appreciate how much it's worth."[49] Addicts like Sheff and Sizemore successfully beat their addictions, but there is no question that the road toward rehabilitation was long and difficult.

CHAPTER 5: How Can Methamphetamine Use Be Prevented?

The illegal heroin trade relies on the cultivation of opium—a crop grown mostly in Asia. As such, the manufacture and transportation of heroin requires the involvement of international drug cartels to distribute the drug in America and elsewhere. To combat the heroin trade, police agencies in many countries are on the hunt for traffickers. The US Coast Guard patrols the shoreline, searching for drug smugglers. Customs agents, accompanied by drug-sniffing dogs, monitor airports as well as the borders very closely.

However, very few of those resources are applicable to the war on methamphetamine. The drug can be made in a basement lab by virtually anybody with know-how and a few hundred dollars to buy the equipment and ingredients. That is a significant reason the illegal meth trade has been able to grow and prosper.

Curbing Cold Medicine

One way in which Congress has tried to crack down on the methamphetamine industry is to regulate the availability of the drug's key ingredient—pseudoephedrine. To this end, in 2005 federal lawmakers enacted the US Combat Methamphetamine Epidemic Act, which places restrictions on the sale of over-the-counter cold and allergy medications that include pseudoephedrine. Products such as Sudafed, Advil Cold & Sinus, and Claritin D can no longer be found on pharmacy shelves; rather, pseudoephedrine-based cold and allergy remedies are stored behind the pharmacy counter.

To purchase the product, the consumer has to request it from the pharmacist. Moreover, the consumer must provide the pharmacist with his or her name and address as well as identification, such as a driver's license. The pharmacist then submits the information to a national database known as the National Pharmacy Monitoring System. It is illegal for a consumer to buy more than 3.6 grams of a pseudoephedrine-based product over a period of thirty days. If the pharmacist learns that the consumer is trying to buy more than the legal limit, he or she is prohibited under law from supplying the medication.

A large box of Sudafed, which includes twenty doses of the medication, contains 2.4 grams of the drug, and a small box contains ten doses, or 1.2 grams. Essentially, then, the law permits a consumer to buy one large box and one small box of pseudoephedrine-based products per month. That is hardly enough to make a profitable batch of methamphetamine, and so meth lab operators have resorted to a number of illegal tactics to procure large quantities of pseudoephedrine.

Smurfing

One way meth lab operators obtain pseudoephedrine is through an illegal method known as smurfing: meth lab operators draft other people, known as smurfs, to enter pharmacies to buy the medications in small amounts. "It's grunt work, yielding little profit and directly exposing practitioners to legal scrutiny,"[50] writes reporter Joseph Tsidulko in the *OC Weekly* newspaper. Smurfs may be friends or even complete strangers. Some lab operators wait outside of pharmacies, offering a few dollars to strangers to buy boxes of pseudoephedrine-based cold and allergy remedies.

Other meth lab operators buy their pseudoephedrine from professional smurfs—people who have obtained dozens of fake IDs. These smurfs drive around all day from pharmacy to pharmacy, buying boxes of pseudoephedrine. In 2013 two notorious professional smurfs, Blanca Bolanos and Concepcion Climaco, pleaded guilty in Orange County, California, to buying pseudoephedrine-based products more than fifteen hundred times over a thirty-six month period. Bolanos and Climaco then sold the boxes to meth lab operators. After pleading guilty, Bolanos was

The combination of inexpensive ingredients and simple procedures for manufacturing methamphetamine is one reason trade in the drug has grown.

sentenced to fifty-two months in a federal prison, and Climaco received a sentence of fifteen months. Writes Tsidulko,

> On a typical day, sometimes with Climaco riding shotgun, Bolanos could hit more than a dozen stores, purchasing from each a box or two of Sudafed or Claritin D—never more than 3.6 grams—after presenting a genuine photo ID. She would later resell the pills at a three-time markup— roughly $10 earned per box. . . . While smurfing might not sound like the day-to-day activity of a major player in the drug business, after Bolanos pleaded guilty to distributing pseudoephedrine, federal prosecutors asked the judge to put her in prison long enough to make you wonder.[51]

Moving Meth Across the Border

Catching smurfs in the act illustrates the challenges law enforcement agencies face as they attempt to disrupt methamphetamine traffic in America. Indeed, for decades law enforcement agencies

Meth Superlabs

Although most American meth labs uncovered by police are small operations that feed the habits of a handful of addicts, police have occasionally uncovered super-labs operating in cities and towns. Superlabs are large operations where thousands of doses are manufactured a day.

One such suberlab was discovered in 2010 near San Jose, California, in a home in the town of Gilroy. Here, police found some 400 pounds (181 kg) of methamphetamine that had been packaged and was ready to distribute to street dealers. The street value of the drugs was estimated at $150 million. This was no basement operation: Virtually the entire home had been dedicated to the manufacture of meth. Quantities of the drug as well as the chemicals used to make it were found stored in kitchen cupboards, closets, and bathroom cabinets. "It's a lot of dope when you start talking about 400 pounds," says Robert Cooke, an investigator for the California Bureau of Narcotics. "That could've messed up a lot of people's lives."

Quoted in Lisa Amin Gulezian, "3 Arrested in $150 Million Drug Bust Near Gilroy," ABC7 News, August 19, 2010. http://abc7news.com.

have relied on such common and usually successful investigative methods as undercover operations and informants to break up drug rings.

Certainly, police still rely on stings to nail methamphetamine dealers. Typically, undercover officers may pose as drug addicts, making purchases from meth lab operators or dealers. After the "buy," the drug is examined at a laboratory to verify that it is methamphetamine. The undercover officers may make several more buys to build their case and learn more about the illegal operation. When, finally, the police believe they have enough evidence to bust the lab operators, they stage a raid. Armed with a search warrant—which is issued by a judge who has seen some of the evidence suggesting illegal activity is occurring in the location of the lab—the police enter, seize the evidence, and make the arrest.

In recent years, however, more and more methamphetamine is being made not in labs in American cities and towns but rather in labs based in Mexico. During the past decade, as some states have legalized marijuana use and others have decriminalized the drug—making possession punishable by just a fine, similar to what a driver would pay for a traffic violation—the illegal drug cartels of Mexico have found the marijuana business less profitable than in the past. As a result, they have turned to smuggling methamphetamine into America.

Now, to stamp out the meth trade, law enforcement officials have focused their efforts on the US-Mexican border as well as efforts within Mexico. In 2012, for example, a raid by the Mexican army near the city of Guadalajara uncovered a major meth lab. Authorities seized some 15 tons (13.6 metric tons) of the drug that were stored in dozens of barrels hidden in the jungle—a quantity capable of supplying 13 million doses to users. Officials of the US Drug Enforcement Administration (DEA) estimated the drug's street value at more than $4 billion. "The big thing it shows is the sheer capacity that these superlabs have," says DEA spokesman Rusty Payne. "When we see one lab with the capability to produce such a mass tonnage of meth, it begs a question: What else is out there?"[52]

> "The big thing it shows is the sheer capacity that these superlabs have."[52]
>
> —Drug Enforcement Administration spokesman Rusty Payne.

El Chapo and the Sinaloa Cartel

Inside Mexico, the arrest of Joaquín Guzmán, known as "El Chapo" (a Spanish nickname that translates to "Shorty"), served to take down one of the world's largest meth producers. Guzmán ran the drug organization known as the Sinaloa Cartel, named for the Mexican state of Sinaloa, where the cartel is headquartered. He was arrested in February 2014 and held in a maximum security prison near the town of Almoloya de Juárez in central Mexico. However, on July 11, 2015, Guzmán escaped from his cell. Prison officials determined that he escaped through a meticulously planned tunnel that was dug by his cartel underlings, who burrowed through the ground from a starting point nearly a mile away. After an international manhunt, Guzmán was found hiding in a Sinaloa house on January 8, 2016. Guzmán was seized during a raid by Mexican marines.

The Sinaloa Cartel smuggles all manner of drugs into the United States as well as other countries, but there is no question that the organization is responsible for a large quantity of the methamphetamine sold in America. In a study of the illegal drug trade in Mexico published in 2013, José Luis León, a researcher for the Autonomous Metropolitan University near the city of Xochimilco, suggested that the Sinaloa Cartel is responsible for as much as 80 percent of the methamphetamine crossing the border. "This organization is a truly global enterprise," León wrote of the Sinaloa Cartel, "for both its markets and its products exhibit a high degree of diversification. North America, Europe, Asia, and Australia stand out among its markets. Marijuana, cocaine, opiates, and methamphetamines are prominent among its products."[53]

After Guzmán's arrest, authorities in the United States announced plans to extradite him—meaning they wanted to bring him to America to stand trial on drug trafficking charges. Mexican authorities commenced negotiations with American officials, stating they were open to sending Guzmán to the United States for trial and eventual imprisonment in a federal penitentiary that could not be breached by confederates tunneling underneath.

The recapture of Guzmán does not mean an end to the Sinaloa Cartel. Guzmán left many lieutenants to run the cartel in his absence. Indeed, while in hiding after his escape, Guzmán had given an interview to an American reporter in which he said, "The day I don't exist, [the drug trade is] not going to decrease in any way at all. Drug trafficking does not depend on just one person."[54] If Guzmán's lieutenants fail to maintain the Sinaloa Cartel's leadership in the international methamphetamine trade, many experts suggest that other drug cartels in Mexico will step in to

> "The day I don't exist, [the drug trade is] not going to decrease in any way at all. Drug trafficking does not depend on just one person."[54]
>
> —Joaquín Guzmán, head of the Sinaloa Cartel.

POLICIA FEDER

Authorities say that drug cartels based in Mexico are increasing their efforts to smuggle meth into the United States. Law enforcement agencies are increasing efforts to arrest members of these criminal organizations.

take over Sinaloa's territory. Steven Dudley, codirector of In-Sight Crime, a public interest group that tracks organized crime in Latin America, says authorities in Mexico cannot rest now that Guzmán has been locked up. "Certainly, there's great value to going after the leadership of the cartels," he says. "You have to illustrate that there's no one who is above the law—that's incredibly important to any country that's trying to build rule of law. But there's a danger of becoming complacent once you eliminate [leaders like Guzmán] when the real fight is still ahead."[55]

Scare Tactics

Despite the success in putting low-level smurfs like Climaco and Bolanos and major drug kingpins like Guzmán in prison, advocates believe American society has to do more than just arrest people to make the methamphetamine problem go away. As

The Smell of a Meth Lab

Meth labs can go into operation virtually anywhere. Because they emit chemical odors, many meth dealers look for remote locations—such as rural cabins—to establish their labs. Others resort to trying to mask the odors. Some lab operators have learned that the noxious odors of the chemicals left over from the meth-making process can be reduced if the chemicals are mixed with ordinary kitty litter. This was what one meth lab in Auburn, Georgia, attempted to do to help hide the odors emanating from its operation. However, the kitty litter did not do a sufficient job in hiding the odors because police discovered the lab after smelling the burning, telltale odor emitted from its operations. Upon raiding the property, they discovered a large-scale meth lab. Auburn police chief Fred Brown reports what they found:

> There was some residue, some beakers of mixtures and some cooking utensils. Other rooms contained buckets of caustic liquids, old containers and garbage bags full of Sudafed tablet packets that had already been popped out of their packaging. Plus in a storage cabinet in plain sight was Sudafed tablets that had been ground up, numerous cans of acetone and charcoal lighter fluid—all the elements necessary to manufacture methamphetamine.

Brown said that the meth makers filtered some of the process's by-products through kitty litter, which was then tossed into the backyard.

Quoted in *Gwinnett Daily Post* (Gwinnett County, GA), "Police Bust Big Meth Lab in Auburn," July 3, 2006. www.gwinnettdailypost.com.

with other drugs, such as heroin and cocaine, years of police work have not been able to stem the illegal methamphetamine traffic.

The New York City–based advocacy group Drug Policy Alliance suggests that in reducing methamphetamine use, government leaders would do well to learn from years of failed attempts to stem the abuse of heroin and cocaine. These efforts, the alliance says, have consisted of efforts to stamp out production in other countries, catch drugs as they are moved over the border, and jail dealers as well as users. "And yet," the Drug Policy Alliance says, "despite spending hundreds of billions of dollars and incarcerating millions of Americans, experts acknowledge that illicit drugs remain cheap, potent and widely available in every community."[56]

For this reason, groups like the Drug Policy Alliance and many government leaders advocate for more effective prevention programs, targeted primarily at young people. Over the years many such efforts have been initiated. Typically, these programs employ scare tactics designed to show young people that methamphetamine can lead to addiction, brain damage, and disfigurement. One such program is Face2Face, which has been used by a number of local communities and school districts. It is a computer program that alters an image of the participant's face, showing how his or her appearance would deteriorate after extensive methamphetamine use. Participants are usually horrified to see their youthful appearance, smooth skin, and bright eyes transformed into a wrinkled, pockmarked and sallow image they barely recognize. "I think that it's definitely an innovative approach in that it's showing the consequences of meth in a very personalized manner,"[57] says Larissa Mooney, a psychiatrist specializing in addiction treatment at the University of California, Los Angeles.

In Semmes, Alabama, the police department installed the program and invites high school students to come in and use it. Hannah Cagle, age seventeen, a senior at Mary G. Montgomery High School in Semmes, found the experience unnerving. "It's not exactly the most gorgeous picture of myself I've ever seen," she said. "It's weird to see yourself look that way. It's a good experience because you never want to see yourself that way."[58]

A similar program is sponsored by the New York City–based advocacy group Partnership for Drug-Free Kids. Known as the Meth Project, the group maintains a website (www.methproject.org) that enables users to see actual mug shots of meth addicts, displaying them alongside portraits of the addicts before they used the drug. Moreover, the website is interactive: visitors try to match before-and-after pictures of the meth users. Visitors often find appearances have changed so much that making correct matches can sometimes be difficult.

The Meth Prevention Lesson

The Meth Project has also designed a program specifically to be used in middle and high schools. Written as a lesson plan for teachers, the forty-five-minute Meth Prevention Lesson provides basic information about methamphetamine and how it is abused, discusses the toxicity of the drug, its effects on the body and brain, and the dangers of using methamphetamine even once. The Meth Prevention Lesson starts with a worksheet that asks students to write down what they know about the drug. The lesson plan includes videos of users describing their personal experiences. The lesson plan is also interactive and seeks to engage students in discussion about the drug.

> "Our goal is to realistically but graphically depict what happens when you use meth. It's not fictitious."[61]
>
> —Alison Metzger-Jones, facilitator of the Montana Meth Project.

Some schools have taken the Meth Prevention Lesson a step further, expanding it beyond its initial forty-five-minute classroom period. In Kahului, Hawaii, students from Kamehameha Maui High School set up a Meth Project booth at the 2015 Maui Fair, an annual event on the island of Maui. "As volunteers, our job was to pass out wristbands and other merchandise to event-goers, encourage people to sign a pledge to stay away from methamphetamine, and tell people about the dangers of drug use,"[59] says volunteer Justin Shiffler II.

In Albany, Georgia, school officials tried a different tactic—holding forums about methamphetamine. In addition to students, parents and other members of the community were invited to attend. One of the speakers at an Albany forum in 2012 was Ralph Craven, who started using methamphetamine at the age of twenty-two. He quickly became addicted and was hooked on the drug for twelve years. After spending a year in jail and beating his addiction, Craven has dedicated his life to warning others about the dangers of meth. Standing in front of an audience of students, parents, and educators, Craven said, "When I was first given meth, I didn't know what it was. It turned me on like a light switch. Whenever I got sober, it seemed like there was an excuse to do it again. It tore my family apart."[60]

Condescending Messages?

Schools often rely on such antidrug tactics as well. In Montana a statewide program called the Montana Meth Project travels from school to school. Alison Metzger-Jones, the facilitator of the project, walks students through the dangers of methamphetamine, showing them videos of teens whose teeth have rotted, or who have picked their skin to the point of bleeding and scabbing, or who have even watched their friends die of overdoses and meth-related violence. "Our goal is to realistically but graphically depict what happens when you use meth," she says. "It's not fictitious. All its stories and information have been gathered from Montanans."[61]

Such scare tactics don't always work, however. The Drug Policy Alliance argues that throughout much of the 2000s, federally sponsored prevention programs focusing on scare tactics

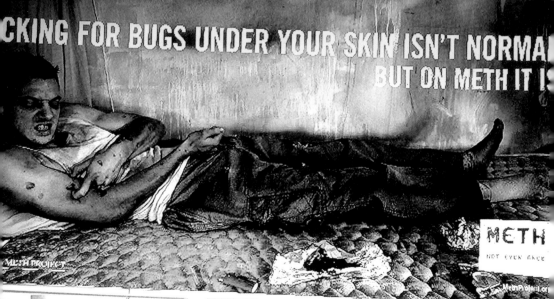

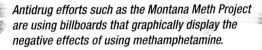

Antidrug efforts such as the Montana Meth Project are using billboards that graphically display the negative effects of using methamphetamine.

have cost some $1.5 billion—and yet the epidemic of meth-amphetamine and other drugs continues. According to the alliance, studies have shown that young people do not react favorably to scare tactics: they find the messages condescending and do not compare their personal situations with the stories told by longtime users. The alliance warns, "Studies show that scare tactics, the over-use of authority figures, speaking condescendingly to young people, and conveying messages or ideas that are misleading, extremist or do not conform with young people's own perceptions and experiences . . . are ineffective and may have a counterproductive effect on the target audience."[62]

> "Studies show that scare tactics . . . are ineffective and may have a counterproductive effect on the target audience."[62]
>
> —Drug Policy Alliance.

Instead, the alliance recommends that to convince young people not to use methamphetamine, dollars would be better spent giving them something more positive to do. "The single most effective way for policymakers to prevent drug abuse among youth is to increase funding for after-school programs," says the organization. In fact, research shows that drug use (and other dangerous adolescent behavior) often takes place between the end of the school day and when parents come home in the evening—when young people are unsupervised. "Increasing funding for after-school programs," explains the alliance, "is especially critical to preventing youth methamphetamine abuse in rural areas, where methamphetamine is heavily concentrated and often where fewer activities are available."[63]

Changing prevention programs from relying on scare tactics to finding productive ways to fill young people's time will likely take some major rethinking on the part of educators, government leaders, and law enforcement officials. In the meantime, police are faced with the enormous task of shutting down meth labs as well as halting the drug traffic that crosses the US-Mexican border. Since methamphetamine use remains a major problem in American cities and towns, the fight against the drug is likely to continue for many years to come.

SOURCE NOTES

Chapter 1: How Serious a Problem Is Methamphetamine?

1. Quoted in Ralph Weisheit and William L. White, *Methamphetamine: Its History, Pharmacology, and Treatment*. Center City, MN: 2009, pp. 157–58.
2. Quoted in Phoenix House, "True Story: Jasmine," July 9, 2012. www.phoenixhouse.org.
3. Elizabeth Fish, as told to Lisa Collier Cool, "Mother's (Dangerous) Little Helper: A First-Hand Account of One Mom's Secret Meth Addiction, and How She Broke Free," *Parenting*, July 2012. www.parenting.com.
4. Quoted in ABC News, "Are Super Moms Turning to Meth to Do It All?," 2015. http://abcnews.go.com.
5. Quoted in Tim Post, "It's Getting Harder to Detect Meth Labs in Minnesota," Minnesota Public Radio, April 15, 2005. http://news.minnesota.publicradio.org.
6. Quoted in *Indiana Economic Digest*, "Indiana Leads Nation in Methamphetamine Busts," April 26, 2015. www.indianaeconomicdigest.net.
7. Malkeet Gupta, Scott Bailey, and Luis M. Lovato, "Bottoms Up: Methamphetamine Toxicity from an Unusual Route," *Emergency Medicine*, February 2009. www.ncbi.nlm.nih.gov.
8. Nicolas Rasmussen, *On Speed: The Many Lives of Amphetamine*. New York: New York University Press, 2008, p. 96.
9. Richard Valdemar, "Gangs on Meth," *Gangs Blog, Police Magazine*, March 14, 2008. www.policemag.com.
10. Nora D. Volkow, "Letter from the Director: Methamphetamine," National Institute on Drug Abuse, September 2013. www.drugabuse.gov.

Chapter 2: What Are the Effects of Methamphetamine Use?

11. Tom Sizemore, *By Some Miracle I Made It Out of There: A Memoir*. New York: Atria, 2013, p. 2.

12. Quoted in *Frontline*, "The Meth Epidemic: How Meth Destroys the Body," February 14, 2006. www.pbs.org.

13. Thea Singer, "Recipe for Disaster," *Frontline*, February 14, 2006. www.pbs.org.

14. Foundation for a Drug-Free World, "The Truth About Crystal Meth and Methamphetamine," 2016. www.drugfreeworld .org.

15. Quoted in Andrew Koubaridis, "Ice Addiction: 'I Was Bonkers.' Former Junkie Tells All," News.com.au, August 22, 2014. www.news.com.au.

16. Quoted in Ken Olsen, "A Health Peril for All of Us," *Spokane Spokesman-Review*, March 3, 2004. www.nbcnews.com.

17. Foundation for a Drug-Free World, "The Truth About Crystal Meth and Methamphetamine."

18. Quoted in *Frontline*, "The Meth Epidemic."

19. Quoted in Meth Project, "Why Are Meth Users So Thin?," 2016. www.methproject.org.

20. Quoted in Olsen, "A Health Peril for All of Us."

21. James Salant, *Leaving Dirty Jersey*. New York: Simon & Schuster, 2007, pp. 279–80.

22. Salant, *Leaving Dirty Jersey*, p. 281.

23. Pima County Office of the Medical Examiner, *Annual Report*, 2013, p. 21. http://webcms.pima.gov.

24. Quoted in US Justice Department, "Report Finds Meth Epidemic in Full Force in San Diego County," November 30, 2015. www.justice.gov.

25. Quoted in Kate Howard, "'I Knew . . . I Would Die a Junkie': Homeless Meth Addict, Considering Suicide, Finds Savior in Grace U Student," *Omaha World-Herald*, December 26, 2014. www.omaha.com.

Chapter 3: How Addictive Is Methamphetamine?

26. Quoted in Tom Robertson, "Meth in Minnesota: The Costly Addiction," Minnesota Public Radio, June 14, 2004. http://news.minnesota.publicradio.org.

27. Quoted in Foundation for a Drug-Free World, "What Is Crystal Meth?," 2016. www.drugfreeworld.org.

28. Quoted in Corinne Reilly, "Why Is Meth So Addictive?," *Merced (CA) Sun-Star*, March 5, 2009. www.mercedsunstar.com.

29. Quoted in Reilly, "Why Is Meth So Addictive?"

30. Steven J. Lee, *Overcoming Crystal Meth Addiction: An Essential Guide to Getting Clean*. New York: Marlowe, 2006, p. 45.

31. Ralph A. Weisheit, "Methamphetamine," in *The Handbook of Drugs and Society,* ed. Henry H. Brownstein. Malden, MA: Wiley, 2016, p. 112.

32. Quoted in Anna David, "A Hollywood Star's Journey Through Meth Hell," *Daily Beast*, September 1, 2010. www.thedaily beast.com.

33. Nic Sheff, *Tweak: Growing Up on Methamphetamines*. New York: Atheneum, 2007, p. 5.

34. Sheff, *Tweak*, p. 270.

35. Salant, *Leaving Dirty Jersey*, p. 85.

36. David Parnell, *Facing the Dragon: How a Desperate Act Pulled One Addict Out of Methamphetamine Hell*. Deerfield Beach, FL: Health Communications, 2010, pp. 181–82.

37. Quoted in Jason Miles, "Parents Charged with Murder After Baby Dies from Meth Overdose," WMC Action News 5, May 7, 2015. www.wmcactionnews5.com.

Chapter 4: What Are the Challenges of Treating Methamphetamine Addiction?

38. Sizemore, *By Some Miracle I Made It Out of There*, p. 167.

39. Sizemore, *By Some Miracle I Made It Out of There*, p. 167.

40. Quoted in Reilly, "Why Is Meth So Addictive?"

41. Adi Jaffe, "Crystal Meth Withdrawal—Not Like Heroin, but Not Easy," *All About Addiction* (blog), *Psychology Today*, May 23, 2010. www.psychologytoday.com.

42. Quoted in Julia Sommerfeld, "Beating an Addiction to Meth," NBC News, 2013. www.nbcnews.com.

43. Quoted in Bill Krasean, "Treatment Offers Hope for Addicts," *Kalamazoo (MI) Gazette*, September 2005, p. 10.

44. Chris Woolston, "Treatment for Methamphetamine Addiction," HealthDay, January 20, 2016. http://consumer.health day.com.

45. David Sheff, *Beautiful Boy: A Father's Journey Through His Son's Addiction*. Boston: Mariner, 2008, p. 207.

46. Sheff, *Beautiful Boy*, pp. 207–8.

47. Sheff, *Beautiful Boy*, p. 211.

48. Robert F. Forman and Paul D. Nagy, *Substance Abuse: Clinical Issues in Intensive Outpatient Treatment*. Rockville, MD: US Substance Abuse and Mental Health Services Administration, 2006, p. 140. www.ncbi.nlm.gov.

49. Sizemore, *By Some Miracle I Made It Out of There*, p. 222.

Chapter 5: How Can Methamphetamine Use Be Prevented?

50. Joseph Tsidulko, "Smurfing Bad: An OC Judge Shows Mercy on Mini Meth-Makers," *OC Weekly* (Orange County, CA), July 25, 2013. www.ocweekly.com.

51. Tsidulko, "Smurfing Bad."

52. Quoted in Damien Cave, "Mexico Seizes Record Amount of Methamphetamine," *New York Times*, February 9, 2012. www.nytimes.com.

53. Quoted in Santiago Wills, "This Mexican Cartel Controls 80 Percent of the US Meth Trade, Study Finds," ABC News, April 2, 2013. http://abcnews.go.com.

54. Quoted in Charlotte Alfred, "Why the Capture Of 'El Chapo' Guzman Won't Stop His Cartel," *Huffington Post*, January 14, 2016. www.huffingtonpost.com.

55. Quoted in Alfred, "Why the Capture Of 'El Chapo' Guzman Won't Stop His Cartel."

56. Bill Piper, *A Four-Pillars Approach to Methamphetamine*. New York: Drug Policy Alliance, 2008, p. 7. www.drugpolicy.org.

57. Quoted in Joseph Brownstein, "Face2Face Computer Program Shows Kids Consequences of Meth Use," ABC News, January 7, 2010. http://abcnews.go.com.

58. Quoted in Brownstein, "Face2Face Computer Program Shows Kids Consequences of Meth Use."

59. Quoted in Gabrielle Constantino, "Hawai'i Meth Project Educates at Fair," Ka Leo o Nā Koa Online, September 30, 2015. http://kaleoonakoa.org.

60. Quoted in Jennifer Maddox Parks, "Forum Points to Dangers of Meth Use," *Albany (GA) Herald*, February 28, 2012. www.albanyherald.com.

61. Quoted in Jamie Kelly, "Montana Meth Project Brings New Campaign to Missoula School," *Missoulian*, March 9, 2012. http://missoulian.com.

62. Piper, *A Four-Pillars Approach to Methamphetamine*, p. 11.

63. Piper, *A Four-Pillars Approach to Methamphetamine*, p. 11.

Drug Policy Alliance

131 W. Thirty-Third St., 15th Floor
New York, NY 10001
phone: (212) 613-8020 • fax: (212) 613-8021
e-mail: nyc@drugpolicy.org • website: www.drugpolicy.org

The Drug Policy Alliance works to establish innovative antidrug programs that focus on education rather than enforcement of laws, prosecution, and incarceration. The alliance's website provides facts and statistics on methamphetamine use. The report *A Four-Pillars Approach to Methamphetamine* is also available on the site.

Herbert House Sober Living

4101 Inglewood Blvd.
Los Angeles, CA 90066
phone: (310) 737-7566
website: http://herberthouse.com

The California-based clean and sober living facility that helped Nic Sheff kick his methamphetamine addiction was founded in 1996. Visitors to the organization's website can take a virtual tour of the facility and read excerpts from *A Beautiful Boy*, David Sheff's book about his son's recovery from methamphetamine addiction.

InSight Crime

American University
4400 Massachusetts Ave. NW
Washington, DC 20016
website: www.insightcrime.org

Founded by former journalists Jeremy McDermott and Steven Dudley, InSight Crime reports on illegal activities in Latin American countries, where the organization believes the mainstream media are often controlled by crime bosses and drug lords who stifle investigative reporting. Many reports on methamphetamine trafficking in Mexico are available on the group's website.

Monitoring the Future

Institute for Social Research
University of Michigan
426 Thompson St.
Ann Arbor, MI 48106-1248
phone: (734) 764-8354 • fax: (734) 647-4575
e-mail: mtfinformation@umich.edu
website: www.monitoringthefuture.org

Each year the University of Michigan's Institute for Social Research surveys young people about substance abuse. The Monitoring the Future website offers statistics, charts, and complete Monitoring the Future reports showing trends in substance abuse among teens. Also, students can read about the methods used by researchers to compile the studies.

Montana Meth Project

PO Box 8944
Missoula, MT 59807
phone: (888) 366-6384
e-mail: info@montanameth.org • website: http://montanameth.org

One of the several state groups to adopt the programs of the national Meth Project program, the Montana Meth Project produces advertisements and films highlighting the dangers of methamphetamine use featuring addicts who live in Montana cities and towns. Visitors to the group's website can watch the documentary *Brain and Behavior*.

Narcotics Anonymous (NA)

PO Box 9999
Van Nuys, CA 91409
phone: (818) 773-9999 • fax: (818) 700-0700
website: www.na.org

NA works with recovering addicts to help them resist the temptations to use drugs. The organization provides mentors and support services for recovering addicts. Visitors to the NA website can download copies of NA Way magazine, featuring stories about addicts talking about their recovery experiences as well as other NA programs.

National Association of Boards of Pharmacy (NABP)

1600 Feehanville Dr.
Mount Prospect, IL 60056
phone: (847) 391-4406 • fax: (847) 391-4502
e-mail: exec-office@nabp.net • website: www.nabp.net

The NABP administers the National Pharmacy Monitoring System, the national database that monitors consumers' use of pseudoephedrine—the main ingredient of methamphetamine. According to the organization's website, pharmacists access the national database more than a million times per month.

National Institute on Drug Abuse (NIDA)

6001 Executive Blvd.
Rockville, MD 20892
phone: (301) 443-1124
website: www.drugabuse.gov

NIDA conducts research into drug abuse in America and also provides grants to universities, organizations, and other groups pursuing drug abuse research. NIDA's website features extensive information on methamphetamine, including statistics on use and health effects. Videos about the drug are available as well.

US Drug Enforcement Administration (DEA)

2401 Jefferson Davis Hwy.
Alexandria, VA 22301
phone: (202) 307-1000 • fax: (202) 307-8320
website: www.dea.gov

The DEA is the federal government's chief agency charged with combating drug trafficking. Visitors to the DEA's website can enter the term *methamphetamine* into the search bar to find numerous reports, speeches, images, transcripts of testimony, and similar resources about methamphetamine.

White House Office of National Drug Control Policy

750 Seventeenth St. NW
Washington, DC 20503
phone: (202) 395-6700
website: www.whitehouse.gov/ondcp

The White House Office of National Drug Control Policy advises the president on drug control issues. Visitors to the agency's website can read about the federal government's High Intensity Drug Trafficking Areas Program, which focuses on halting traffic in methamphetamine and other drugs across the Mexican border.

INDEX

PICTURE CREDITS

ABOUT THE AUTHOR

Hal Marcovitz is a former newspaper reporter and columnist. He has written nearly two hundred books for young readers. He makes his home in Chalfont, Pennsylvania.